10 Sales Tips from the Quintessential Salesperson

(or *How to Avoid Sales Call Foibles That Can Wreck Your Bottom Line*)

By James Howard

This book is dedicated to all the Quintessential Sales People out there, and especially to J.M. who for me was the original.

Copyright 2019 by James Howard

All rights reserved.

Praise for *10 Sales Tips* –

"Man does this book hit home! I see myself and some of my bosses described by you. I like the viewpoint of the customer as there are always salespeople that overlook that key component of the selling process." – C.S., 15 Year Industrial Sales Rep

"A must-read for sales people." – M.O., 25 Year Marine Supplier Sales Rep

"A good laugh…and informative!" – T.G., 20 Year Marine Supplier Area Sales Rep

"I laughed and could see every mistake you poke fun at." – M.C., 12 Year Industrial Sales Rep

"I enjoyed your short book…Good funny tales from the street!" – S.B., 10 Year Beverage Distributor Sales Rep

"Your book makes me laugh…people in the restaurant were turning around to look!" – S.P., 15 Year Marine Supplier Sales Rep

"Loved it…being in a similar position for many years, I can really relate…anyone in a sales position would appreciate this." – G.W., 20 Year Technical Editor and Publisher

"I read your book…full of candor and humor at the same time…sales people need to be trained!" – R.B., 29 Year Paper Products Sales Rep

"This book will be a benefit to salespeople" – C.P., 27 Year Nuts and Bolts Sales Rep

"That book you sent me was hilarious…should absolutely be a top seller!" – C.S., 2 Year Manufacturers Representative

"I love it…a great reference and good solid salesman advice." – D.L., 30 Year Industrial Sales Rep

"Funny and spot on! I was relating a lot of your examples to dealings in my own career." – C.S., 23 Year Marine Parts Manager

"There's a lot to learn from this book…it's going to be a best seller!" – C.L., 7 Year Sales and Marketing Rep

"This book teaches vital people skills for any salesperson. I wish I'd had it when I was starting out!" – M.H., 40 Year Chemical Products Sales Rep

FOREWORD

I am most pleased to write about the abilities and character of the author and my good friend Jim Howard.

I have known Jim for over twenty years and as an outside sales contract supplier for repair parts we had a lot of interaction developing the specifications for parts needed to repair equipment in the entire plant. He prepared a complete purchasing cost savings report for all of the repair items which has been the foundation of the reported cost savings program on a corporate level for both of our companies. This report has helped substantiate the three and one half million dollars in purchasing cost savings.

Jim also accurately organized the myriad part numbers and specifications from various companies and computer systems into a single report for hundreds of pieces of repairable equipment in his facility. This report has been used for many years saving untold hours of research for his fellow employees and parts suppliers alike. In 38 years in the field, I have never met a customer that has helped me as unselfishly as Jim.

The book is a chronicle of observed real life situations about sales calls that the outside salesperson will enjoy reading. Every salesperson needs to avoid the common mistakes the author has so eloquently described and his tips on how to polish the sales call is spot-on. I recommend this book as a humorous and fun must-read for both the new and seasoned salesperson in outside sales. It's short enough to read on the run.

Sincerely, J.M., 38 Year Industrial Parts Supplier

Hello. My name is James Howard.

I am not a salesperson, nor have I ever been a salesperson.

However, I believe that I have a strong history of sales experiences that make me uniquely qualified to write this little book. For you see, I have been a customer.

Allow me to explain.

For many years I was employed, both as a worker and as a manager, of an in-house machinery repair shop in a large industrial facility. Over a million of dollars of parts and equipment flowed through our operation annually and hundreds of sales people called on us over the years.

Some were professional and knowledgeable.

Some were decent but could've used some improvement.

But some, I'm sorry to say, were utterly hopeless.

Every time I would conclude a visit by one of the latter I would inevitably say aloud, "One day I'm going to write a book about salesmanship from the customer's perspective."

And here it is.

Now, I don't mean to sound uppity or conceited toward any salesperson. I'm sure it is a difficult job and is one I'd rather not do.

But in light of the real, true-to-life situations and foibles some salespeople put themselves into, maybe a book such as this might prove useful.

Maybe my experiences can help the hopeless ones after all.

Maybe the decent ones can make some improvements.

And maybe everyone can get a laugh along the way.

After all, the only real categories for salespeople are those who are successful and those who aren't. It's my sincerest hope that anyone reading this material will be more successful.

As to the material itself I must say that every one of the following cases are absolutely, undeniably true.

As ridiculous as some of these stories are, as unbelievable as some of them might sound, they were all actual events I saw with my own eyes and heard with my own ears.

I still have many of their business cards on file and can provide names and contact info (which I will not do).

Who knows? You may even see yourself in these anecdotes.

I will remind you again of the veracity of these stories as we go along.

While these cases represent industrial sales people, I'm sure the lessons learned can be applied to almost any field of sales. I originally intended to come up with only 10 offences and tips, but as I began to write, more and more came to mind. Consider the extras bonus material.

As to the Quintessential Salesperson, there is one salesperson I regarded as the best in the trade and I frequently referred to him by that title.

But frankly, there were others who were of the right stuff also, so for my book the Quintessential Salesperson will be a conglomeration of them all.

I would often confer with them regarding the events which prompted this book so in that sense the tips from the "Quintessential Salesperson" are from real salespeople, sometimes verbatim.

One last note, in the case histories which follow I will describe the offender and assign a false name. I will also relate the offence and its implications before offering the good advice garnered by the Quintessential Salesperson.

I have no desire to give any individual or company a black eye. This book is designed to be humorous and helpful.

I hope these true stories make you smile… and make you *think!*

© www.gograph.com/sparkstudio

Case #1 – Salesperson who promises to bring lunch…and doesn't.

This salesperson is someone we'll call "Dan."

He wears round glasses and a smile that makes you think of Teddy Roosevelt.

He'd recently taken over the territory from another moderately successful salesperson and wanted to get off to a good start.

He didn't.

Some days before he'd arranged to come see me and he offered to bring lunch for the crew. I told him he didn't have to bring lunch but he insisted.

(I don't like taking gifts, even food, from people with whom I'd never done business. To thank us for an ongoing business relationship is fine, but otherwise it looks like a bribe. But maybe that's just me.)

Anyway, he asked us what time we went to lunch and I told him eleven. He asked what we liked and I told him anything was fine. (Our favorite brand is FREE.) He told me he'd bring in lunch the next day at eleven and I informed the crew.

It turned out to be a justification of why I keep a pack of ramen noodles in my desk. He didn't show up at eleven, nor at eleven thirty, but closer to noon - and empty handed to boot!

No one had brought lunch in expectation of the one to be provided, so it was with growling stomachs that we listened to his explanation that since he'd run late, and that since it was already past our normal lunchtime, he'd decided against it.

And then he belched and proceeded to tell us how good it had been.

(Remember, this is a true story.)

The guys left the office to scrounge up whatever they could, grumbling as they went. I took his brochures and got rid of him.

Needless to say, I never did buy anything from him.

The Quintessential Salesperson says – "Don't make promises you don't intend to keep! Better not to promise than to promise and not deliver. If you break your commitment about the trivial things, how can you be relied upon for the important things? Think about it."

Case #2 – Salesperson who wears a college logo on his shirt.

Here is a salesperson we'll call "Charlie" who'd been calling on us periodically for many years. He was one of a pool of salesmen who represented the same company and although his reputation among his peers was dubious, I always liked him well enough.

His folly concerned his enthusiasm for college football.

One day he paid a visit with biscuits in hand and wearing a Clemson Tigers polo shirt.

One of our techs was a deeply committed Carolina Gamecocks fan.

The tech scorned the shirt.

He scorned the salesman.

He even scorned the biscuits, refusing to come in the office and have one until the salesman was gone.

Sound silly? I agree, but it is what it is.

The Quintessential Salesperson says – "Always remain neutral! You are there to serve your clients and make sales, not to brag on your team. Your shirt should have your company logo on it or nothing at all."

Case #3 – Salesperson who tells bawdy jokes and stories of drinking, partying, etc.

We'll call this salesperson "Jim" because he shares a last name with an old time movie star whose first name is Jim.

Jim loved to talk about boozing it up and even had a reference to it on his professional business card. (I believe I still have his card somewhere.)

He seemed to think that blue collar workers would be amused by the talk, and while that is usually a good bet, it is by no means universal.

(In fact, as a salesperson he was not alone in this assumption. There were other salespeople who seemed to think that their partying would make a better lasting impression than their product, and honestly I can't remember what any of them were selling.)

In this case it was a poor bet, for at least two of our crew were religious fellows, including the one who ordered our materials.

Now, I'm not saying that they were offended so they wouldn't buy from him, but what I am saying is that Jim put himself in the same category as the salesperson who comes in with the appalling breath (another true case).

The salesperson might be a great guy (or gal), but their arrival doesn't exactly bring a smile to your face.

The Quintessential Salesperson says – "Get to know your potential clients before you spout off about politics, religion, or amusements. And for Pete's sake, let your fragrances be inoffensive!"

Case #4 – Salesperson who fails to provide a quote.

This may seem to be the most astonishing case so far, but like the others it is absolutely true.

"Bill" was a friend of mine who sold janitorial supplies. Among his products was our favorite heavy duty hand soap and we used a LOT of it.

I was his contact that got him into the facility and also provided names and contact information of others he could call on.

And as he was a friend, I asked him to provide a quote for a few cases of our favorite heavy duty hand soap. I figured I might as well buy it from him as from anyone else.

But instead of giving me a quote so I could order some that afternoon, Bill began to tell me about a new and improved heavy duty hand soap that was much better.

I said, "Ok. Give me a quote for a few cases of that!"

He told me it wouldn't be available for another six months, but he would try to get me some samples.

(True story.)

I asked him again for the quote on the first product and I think I got it about a week later.

The Quintessential Salesperson says – "If your customer wants a quote, then don't leave their office without at least a verbal one. Call your office or inside people if you have to. Then follow up with a faxed or emailed written quote before the end of the day. (And check to make sure they got it within a day or two.) Sell what you can today, then sell whatever new thing is coming when it becomes available."

Case #5 – Salesperson who routinely double orders.

"Cindy" had been a favorite of one of my predecessors and was one of the few women who called on us. I liked her well enough, too, except for one small bad habit.

She routinely double ordered everything.

For instance, if you ordered 10 lengths of 1/2" threaded rod, you'd get 2 shipments of 10 rods each.

The first time it happened she explained that she'd cc'd the home office with my purchase order and they must've mistakenly thought it meant a second order.

Well, since it was a hassle to return the shipment (busy as we were), and since we would use the items eventually, I decided to let it go.

But by the third occurrence I began to see the pattern.

At that point I was sending the items back and it was such a nuisance (and time hog) that I just stopped ordering from her.

The Quintessential Salesperson says – "Remember, short term gains from dishonest or shoddy practices cost you long term, and perhaps more lucrative, sales in the future. Be trustworthy."

Case #6 – Salesperson who makes a sales "call" from 45 miles away.

This was "Charlie" again.

Once in a while I'd get a phone call from him as he was traveling the interstate and would pass the junction for the interstate that headed toward our city.

"I saw the sign for your town and thought I'd call to see if you needed anything."

I'd tell him we were fine and after a little chat we'd conclude the call.

I found out later that after the call he'd log himself a 4 hour stop at our facility. Probably went to play golf instead.

Now, it doesn't matter to me how he is with his employer, but it did make me question anything he was telling me. Also, much of our business was going to folks who were actually calling on us, knew our problems, and were trying to help us solve them.

 **The Quintessential Salesperson says –** "Your reputation is always on the line. You never know who is watching or what they think about how you conduct yourself. Always be professional!"

Case #7 – Salesperson who excessively runs down the competition.

It's remarkable how often I see this, even when dealing with salespeople in my personal life (with cars, appliances, whatever). It's natural to play up the strengths of your products and services, and even to highlight the weaknesses of your competitor, but excessively running down "the other guy" might step on the wrong toes.

"Tom" was bad about this.

"Did you hear about the lawsuit with XYZ competitor?"

"Did you hear about the recall of their such and such model?"

"I heard their products totally failed in such and such environment."

"That salesperson of theirs totally sold one company a lemon, and now is fighting them about making it right."

"Blah, blah, blah…"

Tom never could conceive that we may actually have had good success with that product line. Or that said competitor has been a good resource. Or that said salesperson is someone we really like and/or respect.

But the main point that Tom seemed to miss, the real clincher, was that by running down people and products we liked, he was in effect saying to us, "You people must really be stupid to be buying from them instead of from me."

It didn't go over well.

The Quintessential Salesperson says – "Remember, the other guy is not an enemy, just a competitor. We're all trying to make a buck. If you can't sell your product/service without running your competition down, it might be interpreted that your product/service has no merit. Play your strengths!"

Case #8 – Salesperson who begs for business.

"Chris" came in every so often with products that I had been doing well without, but I might have been willing to take a chance with them if he'd been willing to really sell them.

One day he came in and briefly introduced his product, but before I could ask any questions about it he says, "I don't suppose you'd be willing to buy 2000 or so of these, would you? I'm trying to make my mortgage payment."

Somehow it landed on me wrong.

I have a mortgage to pay, too. We all have problems, but an office during a sales call and possible business transactions is hardly the time or place to discuss them.

Particularly when the tactic is an obvious sympathy ploy.

Perhaps if he'd shown a little more sympathy for the professional problems I was dealing with, he'd have been able to tailor fit his products to them and would've sold 2000 or so.

I'm always open to new ideas, products, and services. One never knows what might make the workload easier. But Chris didn't go in that direction.

His tactic landed on me wrong. Apparently it landed on others wrong, too, for he was told not to call on anyone in our zone anymore.

I suppose his mortgage suffered accordingly.

The Quintessential Salesperson says – "The salesperson is there to serve his customer's needs, not the other way around. Sell the product so that the customer thinks he can't live without it. Then the money takes care of itself!"

Case #9 – Salesperson who makes outrageous claims.

"Andy" was a new salesperson who represented a company unknown to us. And truth be told, almost every product or service we could ever possibly want was already being sold to us by someone else.

BUT, as I'm always on the lookout for better cost, quality, and availability, I give everyone a fair shot. Besides, there's enough business to go around so that I can collect multiple resources for the things we need.

I owe that to my employer.

Andy's business was to weld repair old parts back to factory specs, something we often have done for us. The critical question is, of course, the factory specs.

I need to know if they are familiar enough with the equipment to get it right.

I asked Andy if they ever worked on a particular make and model and he told me that they did all the time.

I asked him to look at one we had and led him out to the shop where a few dozen items lay on pallets on the floor. I waited for him to go right to it, being so familiar, but he looked puzzled.

He was standing right in front of one and didn't recognize it, and my doubts about their precision arose.

Now, I don't expect a salesperson to know everything, but it might've made a better impression for Andy to have called his technical guy.

Too many repair/refurbish people out there seem to think that if they can just get it to their shop, they'll figure out what to do with it.

But that doesn't give me a warm fuzzy feeling, especially when I think of myself rebuilding a piece of equipment at 2:00 am with the production machines shut down costing thousands of dollars a minute and my entire chain of command watching me work and realizing only THEN that the part won't fit.

I hope my treatment of the man doesn't seem harsh, but the fact is with so many sales people coming in with so many exaggerated claims, one must devise means to test them before you spend any money.

My predecessors taught me this.

Shortly after I joined the team we had a salesperson call on us making big claims about a coating product. He held up a coupon of material measuring about 1 inch by 3 inches and about a 1/4 of an inch thick.

He said, "This material is absolutely unbreakable!"

My partner said, "May I see it?" and held out his hand.

The salesperson handed it to him and as my partner took it he said, "Oops!" and dropped it on the floor.

A corner of the coupon broke off and the salesman began to look nervous.

We passed it off, but I don't think we ever bought anything from him.

The Quintessential Salesperson says – "Don't make grandiose claims! Know your products, know your customer's needs, and try to make a fit. In doing so, you will build a good reputation as a good resource."

Case #10 – Salesperson who fails to exude confidence.

"John" was a nice man. Technically speaking he was a marvel.

But somehow he just wasn't a people person.

Everyone liked him, but when he came to tell about his company's service he seemed so deferential and subservient that it made you pity him.

He also had the annoying habit of abruptly walking away during a conversation before you had time to really ask him about what he provided. You'd call him back to ask him a question, but as soon as he'd answered it he was off again.

I asked him about it and he said he was being humble and didn't want to waste people's time, but it came across as a lack of confidence in himself.

After all, his services might save time and money for his customers, but he never stayed long enough to find out how and work that angle.

Which is too bad, because he really did provide an excellent service.

The Quintessential Salesperson says – "If you don't show confidence in yourself, how can you expect for others to have confidence in you? You bring something valuable. When your customer realizes this, they'll thank you for bringing it."

Now let me pause here to say that over all there may be little to differentiate one salesperson from another, but with competition what it is, as fierce as it sometimes is, it may be the little details that spell the difference between on-going success and perpetual struggling. The intent of these cases is to highlight those details.

Case #11 – Salesperson who complains vocally about setbacks.

This case could be easily joined to the one above it as the end result is the same.

"Mike," through no fault of his own, lost a product line.

And that is a true setback.

But by complaining about it every time he came in he began to give the impression that he was washed up.

Then he became a bore.

Truth be told, I've seen several sales people go through this, with various intensities of complaining. I commiserated with them all, and tried to work around the limitation if I could, but at some point every one of them had to move on.

You have to move on.

The Quintessential Salesperson says – "Setbacks are a part of the business. Complain to your spouse, your colleagues, or your boss, but never to your customers. Complaining keeps you focused on the past instead of the future. In fact, by making a habit of constantly discovering new opportunities, you will minimize the

> impact of the setbacks when they
> inevitably come."

On a side note, I saw this principle demonstrated by the Quintessential Salesperson himself.

He'd spent several months collecting dimensions and creating machine drawings for a product which had hundreds of applications in our facility.

He'd even worked a special pricing agreement and it became a very lucrative product line for him.

Then, the manufacturer pulled the line from his sales company to go with another sales group. After all the hard work, someone else would get the gravy.

I spoke to him about it and he said, "Jim, that's just part of the business. Now I need to focus on our other products." And he did.

But since he still had all of the dimensions, and still had the drawings (they were HIS drawings), one of the other companies he sold products for became interested.

Since they sold similar types of products, and since the patent had expired, they began to make units similar to the ones that had been lost. In fact, they made a greatly improved model that became popular.

Now he could sell them to other customers, and when our pricing agreement had ended, he sold them to us as well. And we liked the new style very much.

All this took a few years, but he never lost confidence that all would work itself out.

That's when I started calling him "The Quintessential Salesperson."

Case #12 – Salesperson who likes to gouge if he can.

This one I'll call "Richie."

Now, I realize that pricing can be a ticklish subject, and there are many factors that can affect pricing, including competition. And anyone could expect some variance in price from facility to facility, or even state to state.

But Richie's philosophy seemed to be, "If you can wring 'em, wring 'em."

Our facility tended to get better pricing because we were called upon by many vendors selling different brands of the same type of products, and being technically savvy we could easily discern between true mechanical innovation and snake oil.

Unfortunately, many of our suited brethren in the front office lack such discernment.

Richie also did business with another company in another state which relied heavily on the suited ones to make the decisions (another sales tip for you) and was charging them DOUBLE what he was charging us!

Not a bad gig if you can get it.

Everything was working out right for ole Richie, until the two companies decided to merge and then do a corporate contract for the types of products Richie sold.

(Incidentally, Richie hadn't called on our facility for over 5 years prior to the contract deal. Seems he wasn't interested in our business until a possible corporate deal came up. We weren't amused to see him.)

When the suits began to compare bids, the ones from the other facility in the other state became incensed by how much they had been paying (remember, double).

Not only did Richie's company lose the contract, but the suits didn't want him coming around anymore.

Ironically, they might've fought for him if they'd been getting a decent deal.

The Quintessential Salesperson says – "Always be fair with your pricing. People expect you to make a profit, but not a killing. When your prices are fair consistently you build trust and that translates into long term sales growth."

(As a matter of fact, it was the Quintessential Salesperson's company and product which won the bid. People liked his product and pricing, but they liked him even more.)

Case #13 – Salesperson who ignores the underlings.

"Chester" was an interesting case.

He called on us all the time, but he never said much to the guys working out on the floor.

I guess he figured none of us had the checkbook.

It might've bothered me at the time, but I guess I just figured "it is what it is."

But then we had a promotion and a retirement and then it was me in the office with the checkbook.

After that he would come in all smiles to me, asking me about my family and hobbies, etc. and I remember how it just landed on me funny.

He'd barely give me the time of day before and now he's a boon companion.

It struck me as false and I hate false.

If it wasn't for a corporate contract his company had for their products and services I probably wouldn't have dealt much with him.

The Quintessential Salesperson says – "Take an interest in everyone you meet. Not only is it good for present and future business, but you can gain a lot of useful insight into your customer's needs by listening to the people who are actually doing the work."

(I suspect the Quintessential Salesperson made notes to help him remember details about each one of us (family members, hobbies, etc.) for he asked us about those topics whenever he came in. Taking a personal interest in us made a good impression and we liked him enough to deal with him for decades.)

Case #14 – Salesperson who ostentatiously displays or talks of wealth.

We'll call this guy "Pete."

Pete was a hard worker and began to do really well.

His company did a service for us which was difficult and nasty.

And as I said before, no one has a problem with anyone making a profit, even a handsome profit, but when Pete drove up one day in a super duty, extended cab pick-up truck, complete with a lift kit, oversized tires, and a customized paint job (with a cartoon Confederate General on the door), and it wasn't a company vehicle, people began to wonder if they were paying too much.

Now, it is true that it's no one's business how you spend your money, and no one should make judgments or guesses about how much you make.

But I'm talking about "impressions" made on the customer.

Driving a high-end Mercedes or BMW might make a good impression if you are selling real estate, for given the limited profit margin it says you are a hard worker and a go-getter.

But when you are providing an on-going service with no competition it might look bad.

One day another company came in looking trim and hungry for work and offered to do the same job for less and I don't remember seeing Pete again.

The same thing goes for the guy who talks about trips to watch the masters of the PGA at Pebble Beach, or deep-sea fishing trips, or frequent vacations in the Caribbean.

It might make a good conversation starter in the front office, but you can be sure they'll remember it when the budget cuts come.

The Quintessential Salesperson says – "Be modest in everything – your dress, your ride, and your speech. Appear ready to serve at all times. As with your setbacks, discuss your financial home runs with your spouse, your colleagues, or your boss. Show gratitude only to your customers."

Case #15 – Salesperson hamstrung by lousy inside sales people.

I don't know if every salesperson has to deal with inside people, but many do.

For those of you not familiar with these terms, the "outside" sales people are the ones who actually call on the customer. The "inside" sales people are the ones who assist the outside people by providing technical information, writing up the quotes, and generally facilitating the whole sales process.

A good inside salesperson can make everything run like a well-oiled machine.

A bad one can weaken a company's bottom line and totally wreck an outside salesperson's ability and potential.

"Greg" was an outside salesperson hamstrung by a lousy inside person.

In fact, in every other way he was very much a quintessential salesperson. I suppose that's why he ascertained the difficulty so quickly.

We would discuss his products and I would ask for a quote, and then 2 days later he'd ask if I'd gotten it over the fax or by email and inevitably I'd have to tell him no.

He would never blame the inside salesperson, but I knew that was the problem.

You see, it was the same inside salesperson who had years before tried to bully me into making a purchase order on a quote she'd given me, although I didn't like the price.

It was the same inside salesperson who sometimes jumbled the part numbers.

It was the same inside salesperson whose slipshod habits derailed the careers of more than a few outside sales people.

(The marvel is how such a turkey could survive in a company like that when so many decent sales people had to go.)

But Greg wasn't about to let it happen to him.

As soon as he realized he had to do both jobs the problems cleared up. He worked harder and kept everything going smoothly and I respected him for that. And while he was there, the orders came.

But, as with all good people, he soon left to pursue better employment, and I was happy to deal with him in his new company.

The Quintessential Salesperson says – "Yours is the face the customer sees, not the inside people. Do what you have to do to make things right and tie up all the loose ends before the end of each day. You'll be glad you did."

Case #16 – Salesperson who excessively talks instead of listening to what we need.

"Denny" was bad about this (as was "Bobby" who always sounded like a Southern cartoon character when he talked).

A gregarious salesperson is far better than a quiet one, but conversation is supposed to be a two-way street.

Denny would listen to about a half a sentence from you before launching into a fifteen minute blather about how he'd helped another person with a similar issue.

The problem was that he really didn't listen long enough to find out the exact details of our issue, so typically his advice was of little value.

He did the same thing when getting to know the other folks on the team.

For example, as soon as he'd hear the word "fishing" come up in a conversation he would launch into tales about his fishing trips, or trips from people he knew, etc.

Frankly, I found him boring.

And I knew that by the time he left he knew no more about me or my professional difficulties or needs than when he came in.

The Quintessential Salesperson says –
"Take an interest in your customers and

you will find out what they need, then you can apply your products or services to meet those needs. And remember, just like in dating, you make people feel comfortable around you when you let them talk. By listening, you earn the right to pitch your wares."

Case #17 – Salesperson who deals corruptly.

Now this is such a ticklish subject that I won't even assign a false name.

The problem is that corruption can be hard to identify unless it's brought to you directly.

But make no doubt, corruption carries with it a distinct aroma.

(Perhaps it's like cigarette smoke on your clothes. A non-smoker can smell it on you faster than a smoker can.)

When you see a salesperson new to the territory suddenly getting a lion's share of the business, or when you see a salesperson holding onto business for years despite repeated product or service failures, or when you see a salesperson consistently getting higher prices for his products or services than his competitors get for their comparable ones, then there's a good chance that someone somewhere is getting a kickback of some kind.

I didn't really want to include this case, but as it seems so prevalent throughout the industry I realized that I needed to.

The problem is that the money and the edge over competitors can be so tempting.

But the repercussions can be lethal.

Take the case of the "unnamed salesperson."

He arrived with a reputation of being "thrown out" of at least three other facilities.

I didn't like some of his other mannerisms (found in previous cases) so I never really dealt with him, but others did.

Corrupt sales people can always seem to find those with whom they can conduct their kind of business.

And while the bottles of expensive liquor, the premium shotguns, the deep-sea fishing trips, and the masters' series golf tickets, etc. may seem like just innocent thank you gestures prior to actually receiving business from said customers, there is a price to be paid for such shiny baubles.

Sadly enough, it's the receiver's employer who actually pays for them in the short and in the long run, not only because the price of the product or service will be adjusted to cover the bauble, but the decreased fair competition will rob the company of the best cost, quality, and availability.

And in that sense it's fair to say that the receiver is in reality STEALING from his own employer.

But since this is a book about being a better salesperson, and not a book about ethics, I'll put the further implications to one side.

There are several problems that can arise from dealing corruptly.

One is that the receiver may continue to raise his or her price (shinier baubles, etc.). Once you start that line of work, each side has the other over a barrel, so to speak.

Another problem is that the receiver may be transferred or retired, and their successor might resent the special business relationship you had.

But I think that the worst scenario is where the receiver is found out in his practice of violating his company's ethics rules.

He is given a moral black-eye and is fired or demoted, and you receive a matching black-eye and are instructed not to return to the facility, or worse, not to return to any of the company's facilities.

You might believe that others observe the corruption to be congenial and natural, and you may think that others in the company will look out for you when things go sour, but make no mistake, once someone is fired everyone will turn on you with attitudes of morality and piety.

It's just human nature, and in the end the risks of corruption just aren't worth it.

The Quintessential Salesperson says – "Honor is a gift a person gives to themselves. The corrupt parties on both sides will inevitably fall and when that happens the short term gains will be nothing compared to the steady long-term losses. Trust makes solid business relationships and that converts to long term prosperity for all sides."

Case #18 – Salesperson who only wants to make money (as opposed to the ones who sometimes help with no profit to themselves).

I saved this one for last because over the years this one has proved most important of all.

In fact, every salesperson I know who I would regard as a Quintessential Salesperson has taken the high road on this issue.

To be honest, I can't think of anyone who would resent a salesperson who only comes through when it is of direct benefit to themselves.

After all, a salesperson's time is limited, and they have to make a living like everyone else. It's perfectly acceptable that they should tend to business that is mutually profitable.

BUT, the one who takes time to help you out when you are in a bind, to no benefit to themselves, garners the highest gratitude, respect, and loyalty.

For instance, the salesperson who provides drawings and/or dimensions for his equipment so I can buy an add-on product that he doesn't sell, or the salesperson who helps me identify and inventory his old products on our shelves, thus saving us money by preventing us from buying items we already own, or the salesperson who, when he finds out we need something that he doesn't sell, puts us into contact with someone who does sell what we need.

All of these garner the highest loyalty, for they were there when we needed help, with no benefit to themselves.

Now I know some of you might point to the last one and think, "He probably got a finder's fee for that sale," and you may be right.

But if he did, I never heard of it.

The impression I got was that he helped me to no benefit to himself, and in the sales business impressions count.

As a customer, the impressions I got were,

1) This salesperson is a valuable resource.
2) This salesperson cares about my difficulties.
3) This salesperson wants to help me succeed.

I am always glad to see that salesperson come through the door.

I will always take time to hear about their newest product or service.

I have total confidence when I refer this person to a boss or colleague.

I will go to bat for this person when the chips are down.

(Perhaps not everyone will, but most would do so.)

The Quintessential Salesperson says – "Like honesty, a reputation for taking care of your customers' needs builds trust, solid business relationships, and long term mutual prosperity."

I hope you have enjoyed this little instructional booklet written from a customer's perspective and I thank you for reading it.

I hope it has made you smile and I hope it has made you think.

If you have any other tips or anecdotes, please share them online at <u>quintessentialsalesperson.com</u> .

By simply taking the time to read this far you have proved that you are open to new ideas and you're willing to improve your skills. These are the basic traits that make for a successful Quintessential Salesperson and I believe you will go far in the trade. I wish you all the luck, success, and prosperity there is.

Sincerely,

James Howard

© www.gograph.com/sparkstudio

To buy copies of this book in bulk at a discount, contact the author at quintessentialsalesperson@gmail.com . Please state how many copies you want and the address to which you want them sent. Payment can be made to his PayPal account at james.howard75@yahoo.com.

Thank you!

www.ingramcontent.com/pod-product-compliance
Lightning Source LLC
Chambersburg PA
CBHW022000290426
44108CB00012B/1154